Light, Photography Understanding and Practice by Jason S. Page

Light

Practical Guide to the Understanding and Practice of Photography

by Jason Page
Inspired from Danielle Dorsey

**ISBN-13:
978-1725556775**

**ISBN-10:
1725556774**

Copyright Jason Page 2018
First Publishing, August 18 2018

Page Telegram Publishing, pagetelegram.com

Light, Photography Understanding and Practice by Jason S. Page

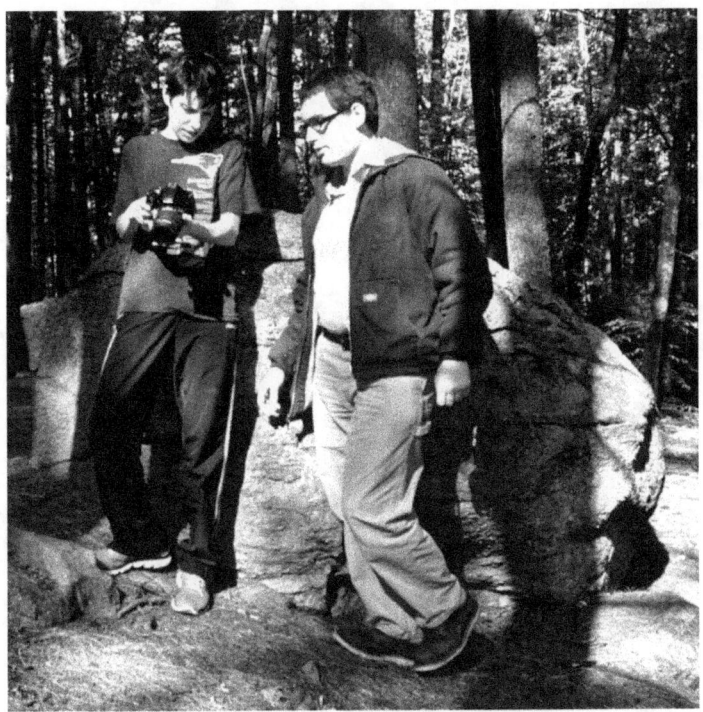

(Pictured: Danielle and Jason, taken May 29th 2014)

This book is dedicated to my dear friend Danielle Dorsey, prepared for her 30th birthday, whom we both have had the pleasure to share memorial times behind the lens of light. She gave me the idea to create this book and I ran with it! It has been so many years that we have known each other and she still surprises me. Even though we live so far apart demographically, we still keep in touch on a regular basis. She knows me better than myself sometimes and I learn about myself more by reading between the lines with our dialogue.

My friend Christopher Mitchell told me months ago that he wanted to learn photography so this book is also written for him and anyone else that would like to learn photography in understanding and practice.

Light, Photography Understanding and Practice by Jason S. Page

1a. Understanding Digital Sensor and Film Photography with Light

In the market place today, digital has claimed dominance while the fringe of film is largely limited to B/W photography. Back when film was the dominance in the market there was black and white and color options. The options included the grade as well as the sensitivity. There were negative and positive films. Positive films were limited mostly to slide film where a projection of light through the film would project the image to a screen or wall where negative film would project the image with colors inverted.

The sensitivity of the film was measured in ISO. Generally the lower the ISO the more light is needed to produce a quality image. The higher the ISO the more grainy the image comes out. This is the same with digital cameras.

The grade of the film determines the quality that can be achieved and are categorized by resolution (how fine the grains) and the dynamic range of the color as well as color preference such as films specific to different hues of output when processed.

In the digital realm of sensors the grade depends on the quality of the sensor. And there are two material types of sensors: CCD and CMOS. Most digital cameras today you will want to go with CMOS sensors as they have been more developed to provide better color dynamic range even though they generally require slightly more light. Today the difference in light requirements between CCD and CMOS sensors is close to no difference making the CMOS the dominant market format for sensors. More important than the resolution or how may mega-pixels the camera is able to achieve is the sensor size. A small sensor size will cause fringing and a lot of garbage pixels. So if you are shooting at a high mega-pixel rated camera that has a very small sensor size, then most of that pixel information is just "garbage" noise and it be better off shooting at a much lower mega-pixel with that camera to achieve practical results. Generally professional cameras have at least a sensor size of the APS size which is just smaller than full frame 35mm size. And there are camera bodies that accept both digital and film medium format sizes. The size of the sensor determines the price as larger sensors have a greater waste per production output when manufactured. Also grade depends on the light mechanics of the sensor. Most sensors are single layered called bayer, where each pixel location captures either a green, red or blue value of light intensity and not all three at each pixel location (referred to mosaic method.) This bayer type sensor requires processors to "make up" color information that is not captured and this often can cause moire patterns in pictures that have a lot of closely drawn lines that are high contrast from each other such as a photo of someone wearing a checkered or striped shirt. To date, the only camera make that produces a sensor that captures full color light at each pixel location is Sigma of Japan. They bought a sensor company that produced their sensors of the SD9, SD10 and SD14/15 cameras to produce their flagship camera the SD1. That company was called Foveon which is from the Latin word Fovea meaning "Eye." See the book "The Silicon Eye" by George Gilder which details the story of the Foveon sensor and it's early development with the help of Carver Mead.

*

C2a. Operation of Light Before Light Reaches the Film or Sensor

There are two functions of light: the intensity and the focus. Two functions control the intensity: The shutter speed and the aperture. The shutter speed is how long light is allowed to hit the film or sensor. The aperture is a measure of how wide the opening is for the lens that allows light to come in, which is also called the F-stop measurement. Two functions support the focus: The aperture and the focal length. There are in manual lenses a ring for focal length as well as a ring for aperture. On automatic and digital Single Lens Reflex cameras the aperture maybe controlled electronically. In such cases you can have either Manual control, Aperture Priority Mode or Shutter Priority Mode. In Manual Mode you need to meter and set your aperture and shutter separately. A faster shutter speed can be used for scenes that have a lot of light in order to allow you to use a smaller opening for the aperture. Aperture can also allow you to control the depth of field of your focal point.

The smaller the opening of the aperture the more depth you will have in focus, however that will require more intensity of light. Some lenses produce different qualities and effect for the blurriness outside the range of your photo subject or object focus. This quality is termed Bokeh borrowed from the Japenese meaning of blur or haze (ボケ / bo-ke).

On the operation of shutter speed you want to use a faster shutter speed for movement and slower shutter speed for low light non-movement, unless you are going for a trail or motion blur effect.

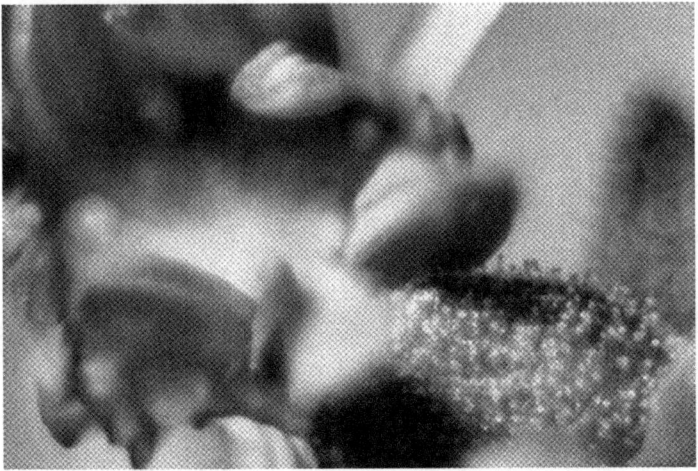

(Macro with 42mm Helios Lens and Bellows, Sigma SD9, 2007)

Interlude:

The following short chapters are examples of how you control the flow of light in different scenarios in practice. Everything you read in the first two short chapters should be enough for gaining an understanding of the practice. With practice you should no longer need the examples and you'd eventually be able to get quality photos in any given scenario provided that you have the appropriate equipment and sufficient amount of light. This book will not detail circumstances that require artificial light such as a flash or studio light as those functions are not the scope of this teaching. Rather this teaching is to give you grounding in the ability to make use of what ever light you have to work with as the scope of this book is on practicality and not idealism.

Light, Photography Understanding and Practice by Jason S. Page

Chapters for Practice:

C1b. Landscape, sun position and accounting for clouds; Sunsets and Sundowns

C2b. The Moon

C3b. Insects and Insect portraits

C4b. Birds in Trees

C5b. Flying Birds

C6b. Going to the Zoo

C7b. Flower Fields

C8b. Individual Flower(s)

C9b. Self/Portrait: In/Out-door

C1b. Landscape, sun position and accounting for clouds; Sunsets and Sundowns

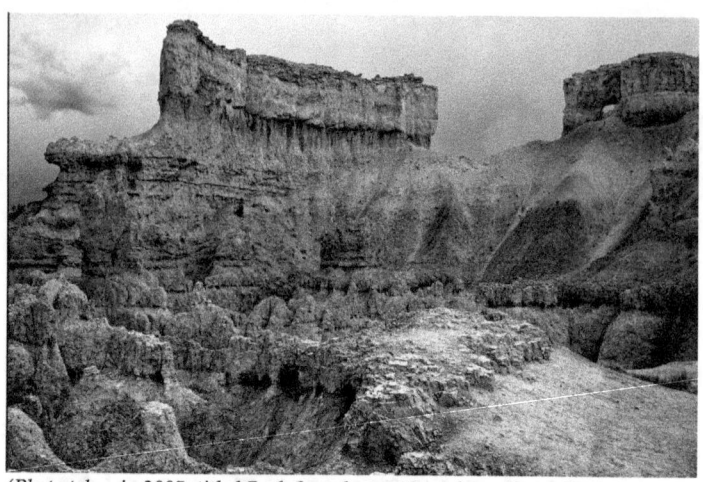
(Photo taken in 2005, titled Rock Symphony, 18mm lens, Sigma SD9)

Most landscapes you want to use a wide angle lens. Zoom lenses can be optional if the range is fitting anywhere between 18mm and 70mm. You are best wide as wide as 18mm-24mm than zoom such as 70mm. This is because you want to reserve the zoom for focusing while moving closer or further way from the scene for your ideal framing.

First you want to get in the correct position. If the sun is beaming at you at your desired position then you better waiting until the sun is either directly above you or somewhere behind you. Note that if the sun is behind you you want to negotiate framing so that no shadows of anything behind you or even your body are being casted in your scene.

Sometimes you want to get a scene with the sun at the horizon in your landscape photo. You want to wait until the sun is just below the horizon and as such you will see beautiful colors of light in the sky as part of your scene.

Clouds can also help in your scene to both diffuse the light extremes to allow the light to be equal in intensity as well as provide more elements of joy to the eyes in the photo.

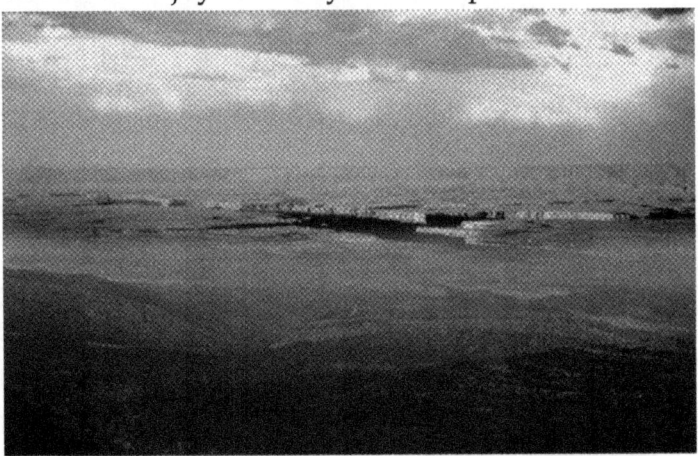

(Grand Canyon, 2005: 18mm, Sigma SD9)

For focusing when you are using a zoom lens you want to get in position of framing where the lens is zoomed out the most. Now when you have your preferred framing of the scene, zoom all the way into the subject you wish to have in focus. Then turn the focus ring and hold the shutter half way until you here a beep or see the light in the viewfinder indicating that the object is in focus. Then leaving your focus ring untouched you can safely zoom out and go back to your desired framing.

If you have in your photo a big range between bright and dark, you will want to save your file as RAW or 16bit TIFF, with the RAW option preferred. The reason for this is that RAW and 16bit store more of the dynamic range of your photo and will allow you to use tools to bring in and out those high and low light intensities within an ideal range for export to either jpeg or png for sharability.

If you are using film then you want a film that as high dynamic range. Usually the lower the ISO the better the range however keep in mind that lower the ISO also means the more light is needed to expose the film. You may consider slide film as a film alternative as that film tends to have higher dynamic range and vibrant colors.

Settings for sensitivity and light you want to have low ISO and aperture as priority while leaving the shutter to auto as there should be plenty of light in your landscape scene to accommodate. Shutter you want as low as possible however no lower than 100th/sec unless you are using a mono-pod or a tripod then you can safely go lower. If the sun is above you or below you it is fine if your shutter speed is much faster than 100/sec.

Light, Photography Understanding and Practice by Jason S. Page

C2b. The Moon over the Water and Moon as a Subject

In this situation you want to frame the moon in a constellation when the moon is close enough to the horizon of the body of water while still having the size of the moon big enough to show some of it's detail. You also want to meter your exposure to the brightness of the moon. You also need to use a tripod, and depending on your stability you might get a way with using a mono-pod.

You will want the ISO low as possible or native ISO to the camera's sensor (usually native ISO is 100 which is perfect) so any range between 100 and 400 is good. Using any ISO larger than or equal to 800 ISO will produce very grainy results. Some digital cameras such as Fuji makes use sensors that are better in low light. If you are using a Sigma SD camera it is safe not to go above 400 ISO.

With the lens you may want to use anything that is between 24mm and 50mm. Usually this range is referred to as a portrait lens.

When the moon and lake is in relation to your ideal framing for what you want, set your camera on a tripod and keep the shutter as slow as possible while adjusting the aperture until the moon detail is within visible range.

You may want to set the timer on your camera if it has a timer for the shutter as pressing the shutter can cause a motion blur in this scene, making the moon blurry. If your camera does not have a shutter timer you can check to see if there is a port for either a mechanical or digital shutter release. Some newer cameras have a shutter relies that is wireless. Some of the older remotes used Infrared (IR) remotes where you have to be in line of site with the camera's IR sensor for the remote to work. However newer wireless designs have incorporated the blue-tooth protocols so you can remote the shutter from anywhere within close range of the camera.

With moon as a subject, you want to use a zoom lens and get as close to the moon as your zoom would allow. Everything else discussed is the same. Typical zoom ranges for moon as a subject are 500mm to 1200mm. These lenses can be very expensive and are referred to as telephoto lenses. Some telephoto lenses are also zoom lenses, however the quality is compromised by the extra glass that is required to give it the optical zoom feature.

Also if your camera has the Mirror Up or Lock option, that is in Single Lens Reflect Cameras, the camera will not shake due to the mirror action moving up and down. This is important when you are dealing with low light, low ISO and slow shutter. And you most definitely want to use some kind of shutter remote, either wired or wireless. I know the Sigma SD9 camera has a connector that is both digital and mechanical, so both mechanical and digital remotes work on this Foveon camera. Most modern dSLRs use digital remotes or wireless when film SLRs use mechanical shutter releases.

C3b. Insects and Insect portraits

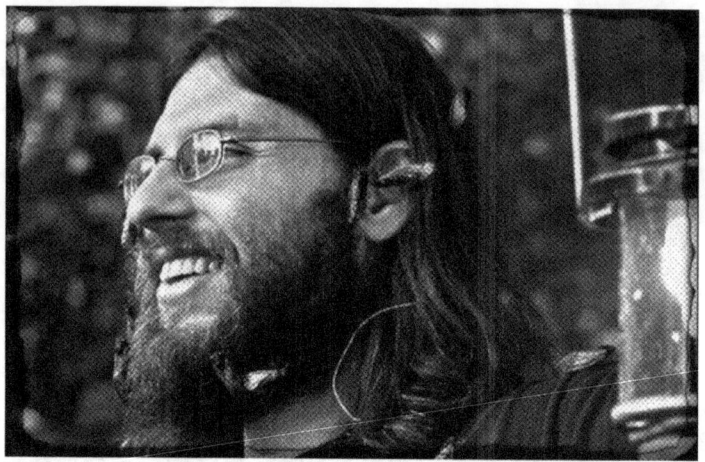
(Taken in 2007 with 105mm macro lens, Sigma SD9)

You will need a Macro-lens which is a fixed focal length with a focus ring with tele-optics. Usually a range of 105mm to 150mm Macro is ideal. Alternatively and sometimes with better results you can use a bellows with a standard portrait type lens (30-50mm.) They can be affordable if you go with old manual lenses with the old standard M42 screw mount. Such good lenses for the most bang for the buck are Soviet era Helios M42 lenses.

If using the bellows, extend it as far as it would extend then use the focus ring to adjust focus. Using a mono-pod is ideal as it will make it easier to maintain focus as any small movement will also move your focal point away from the insect.

Shutter speed and Aperture are not as crucial so shooting in Automatic or Program mode is fine. You will want to pay more attention to keeping the subject in focus and you will want to be very close to the insect, especially for insect portraits.

Different insects exhibit different habits and behaviors. I will go over the most common types.

- Butterflies are usually unaffected by slow movements. It is only quick movements that will cause them alarm and hence fly away. Bees and bumble bees share a similar behavior.

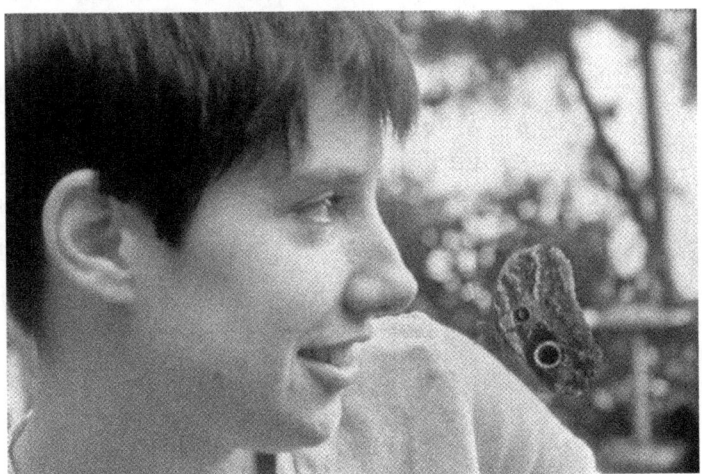

(Butterfly landing on Danielle, 2012, 18mm lens, Sigma SD14)

- Dragonflies are alarmed with any movement, especially as you will want to be very close to them. However they are also habitual to preference. They will most likely always return to their point of place. So if you see one on a flower, as you move closer it will fly away. Position yourself as close as possible and use a tripod as that will prevent any unnecessary movement. Just sit and wait for the dragonfly to return to it's habitual place. You may then only have to move the head of the tripod to get the dragonfly in frame. Use extremely subtle movements. If your movement alarms the dragonfly again just be patient and wait again for it's return.
- Some flying insects like cicadas and locusts are generally not alarmed with movement, to the point where you can actually pick them up and place them where you want them to be in the photo. In the example photo above I poured cicadas over a man with a big bushy beard before taking this shot.

Be clear of any shadows. Sometimes if the sun is directly behind you there will be many shadows casted from your body to the leaves of any plants and limbs of any insects. Best time to get the insects is early morning.

With good practice with these insects portraits and photos you can gain comfort in setting aperture and shutter speeds manually.

When it comes to framing the insect, the quality of how our eye flows when looking at a photo is the rule of 1/3rds. Horizontally you will want to frame the insect or subject 1/3rd in the frame, never dead center 1/2. The reason this is aesthetically pleasing has to do with how all natural elements grow in a progress of the Fibonacci sequence and the rule of thirds conforms to this nature with the Golden Ratio. So you can just say 'it is in our DNA.'

C4b. Birds in Trees

You will want a tele-photo lens of at least 300mm. You can get away with 150mm if you are outdoors and wait for them to land close to you on a tree branch. Be as close to the branch of the tree as possible when keeping a level plane with them. Using a ladder or climbing a nearby tree may help you get close, however do not get too close as most birds know your presence and don't know your intent. Ideally a tele-photo lens of 500mm-800mm is ideal, especially if you are shooting from a window in your bedroom for example. Doing so you will want to setup on a tripod and use a remote or shutter release as any slight movement can cause the exposure to be blurry. Mirror up and lock is not necessary as there is enough light to maintain a fast enough shutter speed. You can shoot in Automatic / Program mode.

When it comes to framing the bird, the quality of how our eye flows when looking at a photo is the rule of 1/3rds. Horizontally you will want to frame the bird or subject 1/3rd in the frame, never dead center 1/2. The reason this is aesthetically pleasing has to do with how all natural elements grow in a progress of the Fibonacci sequence and the rule of thirds conforms to this nature with the Golden Ratio. So you can just say 'it is in our DNA.'

C5b. Flying Birds

This is probably the most difficult task. I remember when I was trying to photograph dragonflies mid-air and in close range. After about 120 shots, only one of them was usable. It was good practice, kinda like when the guru in the Karate Kid was trying to catch flies with chop sticks. However with birds at long range where their direction can be somewhat predicted, the task of photographing them can be more or less attainable and with practice you can usually get a usable shot within the first try. If it takes three tries, you can call that a birdy; well at least that's what they call it when Golfing.

You will want to have a tele-photo lens of at least 300mm, although 500-800mm would be ideal. Try to shy from zoom lenses as they provide less quality optics since more glass (or sometimes worse, plastic) lenses are used. You can usually tell the quality of the lens by how low the aperture can go. Some Zeiss lenses can go as low as an f-stop of 1.2. They can be very expensive yet lenses that go as low as 1.8 or 2.0 are more reasonably priced and common indicator of good optics. Zoom lenses usually are around an f-stop of 3.5 and that's and indicator of bad optics as the light becomes weaker before reaching the sensor or film. So try to stick with fixed focal length in lens choice. Having one zoom lens in your collection such as a 70mm-300mm at 3.5 f-stop is sufficient for having the flexibility however it will be inferior to your fixed optic collection.

When you see a bird flying, try to spot it in your viewfinder. And use a shutter speed of at least 1/500 to 1/1000 with aperture priority. Use manual focus as time is of the essence and auto-focus tends to take time and not always focus right as it drains your batteries. Once your focus is set, frame just ahead of the direction the bird is flying and having your dial in burst mode in order to take a sequence of 3-6 shots in a short amount of time. Decide from the 3-6 frames which one you want to keep and according to the 1/3 rule and delete the rest.

C6b. Going to the Zoo

Keep in mind that zoos can get very crowded and animals are so much at a safe distance that the single most important lens will be a telephoto lens of at least 300mm however 500mm maybe preferred. Keep a portrait lens with you just for getting photos between friends and family members that go with you.

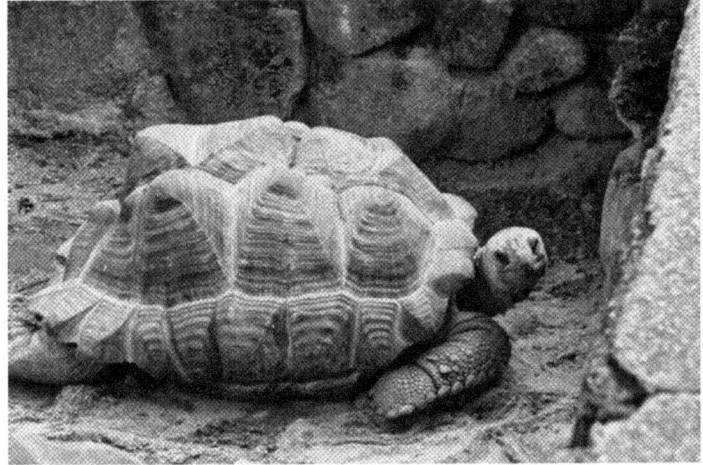

(Southwick's Zoo, MA: 300mm Lens, Sigma SD14)

When it comes to taking photos through mesh-styled fencing, you will want to be in manual focus as auto focus will be confused between the mesh fence and the subject you are focusing on. With a telephoto the mesh will conveniently disappear with the focal length on the animal.

When shooting through glass you also want manual focus and make sure if you have a pop-up flash that you have "no flash" setting turned on. A flash will most definitely obscure your photos and the photos will not be usable with a flash used over glass.

Also a flash especially pop-up flash is unsuitable for lenses that are tele-photo (100mm and above) even at 70mm you are not making good use of the pop-up flash.

Using a flash in daylight is only effective as fill light for B/W photography. Keep in mind that the color temperature of the sun and that of the flash are different and will mess with the color quality of the photo which is why you need professional lighting with gels and color filters for those lights to do the job right. And that is an entire study of Understanding and practice of itself that goes beyond the scope of this book.

Light, Photography Understanding and Practice by Jason S. Page

C7b. Flower Fields

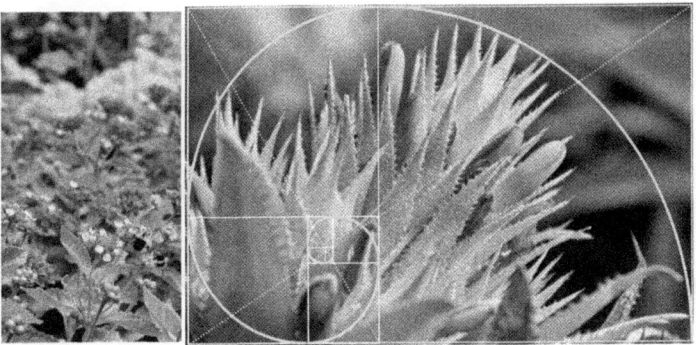

(2015, lenses 18mm and 105mm macro, Sigma SD14)

You will want mostly a wide angel lens and also a fish-eye lens as capturing a large area from a close up vantage point maybe desired. Ideal conditions is during the daytime, sometimes in morning and at dusk where the sun is behind you when taking the photos.

An example of a fish eye is you frame the view according to the 1/3 rule where the subject of focus, being a single flower can go out into the other 2/3rds of the frame begin the field of flowers. Above is a photographic example with the 1/3rd line drawn over the photo as an example. A fish eye lens is any lens that is less than 18mm wide. So anything from 8mm to 16mm are considered fish-eye lenses. The smaller the number the wider and more area that is covered. Just be mindful also that the smaller the number the more rounded the captures will be.

A wide angle lens is anything 18mm to 30mm and you can use it to shoot from a distance to cover any amount of area you want. You might prefer on setting the framing on a slight angle to allow the eye to flow. Straight and centered photos without a focus on direction or subject can not be very appealing to the eye. Some may describe such photos as boring or uneventful. This again is because the eye has no where to focus or travel.

Light, Photography Understanding and Practice by Jason S. Page

C8b. Individual Flower(s)

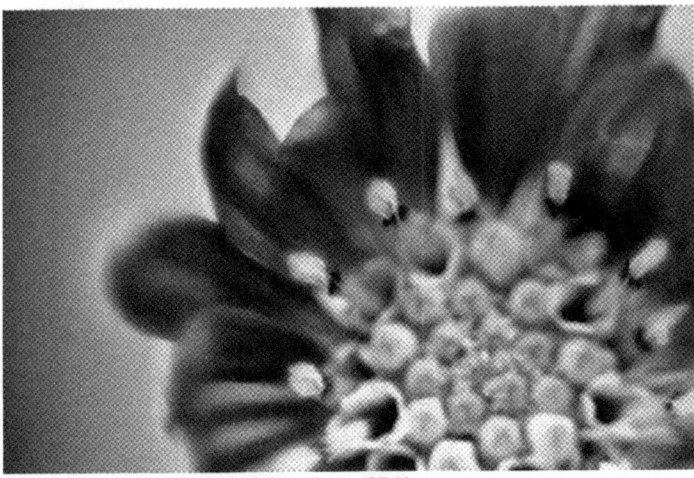
(2007, Bellows with 42mm Helios, Sigma SD9)

You will want to use a Macro Lens such as a 105mm or 150mm for individual flowers. If you wish to just get an extreme close-up of any features of a single flower then you may use a bellows to achieve that with the bellows fully expanded, the lens very close to that feature until the feature appears in focus.

Another trick that photographers use for visual appeal is to use a spray bottle or a mist bottle to spray water droplets onto the flowers you are photographing. This gives the flowers character.

Light, Photography Understanding and Practice by Jason S. Page

C9b. Self/Portrait: Indoor & Outdoor

In the final chapter is portraits. You will want to use a lens that is somewhere between 30mm and 50mm. A Helios 40mm lens is ideal for the quality of the bokeh (blurriness) has character.

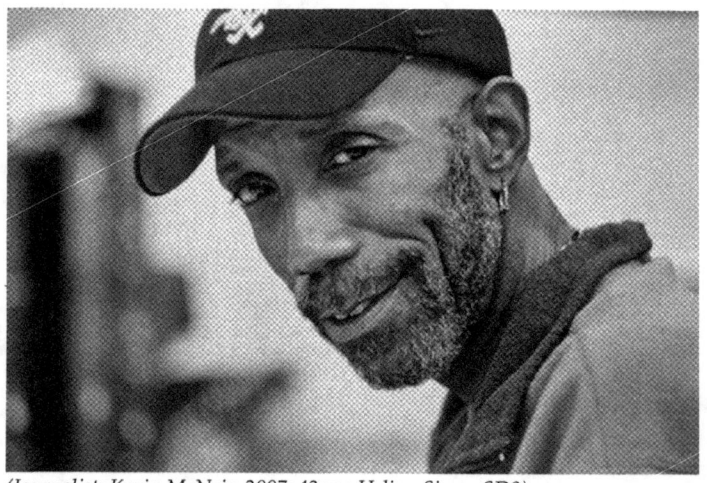

(Journalist: Kevin McNeir, 2007; 42mm Helios, Sigma SD9)

The 1/3 rule also applies to portraits. You do not want the person to be dead center as the eye in such photo would not have anywhere to flow with what is called negative space. Negative space is the area that is not your subject or focus.

Keep in mind of what you want in the background of the portrait and prop that. If indoors you want to make sure what ever light you have that the face of the subject is properly lit. If they have glasses or a hat on then you may need to lower the light source so shadows do not cast below their glasses or hat. You may decide in this situation to use your pop-up flash as a fill light. You can also diffuse the pop-up flash with either a professional diffuser (ie Gary Fong) or cut one out of a half gallon jug from a milk container and tape it to cover the flash. Direct flash can create blow outs especially since you will want to be close enough for the fill light to be effective so diffusing the light is recommended.

Fill diffused light used with flash, Indoors:

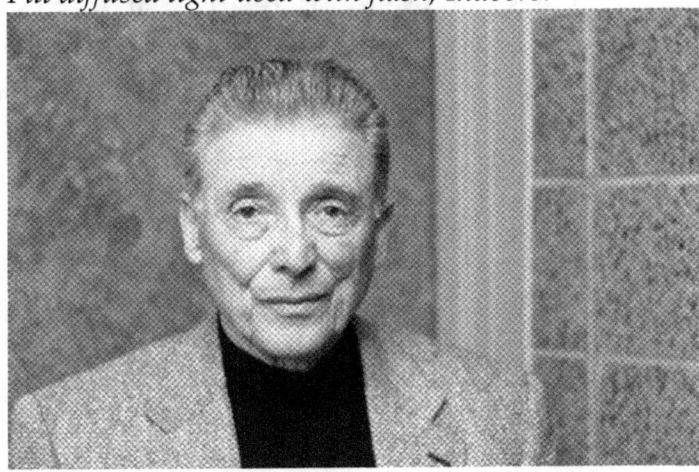

(Aaron Elster, Holocaust Survivor, 2005; 18mm, Sigma SD9)

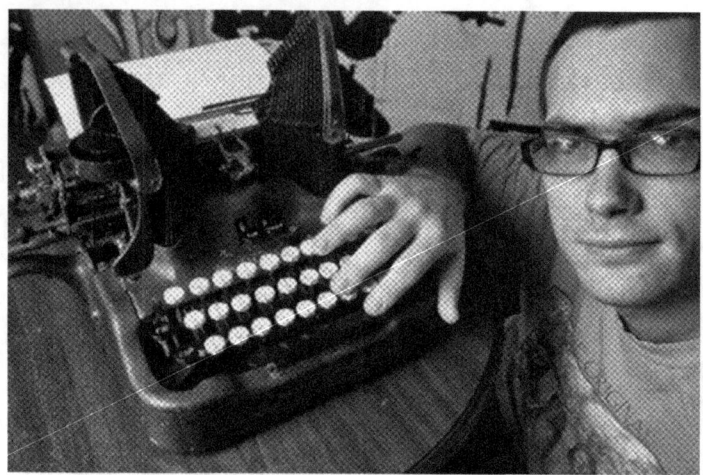

(Jason Page with Oliver Type 9, 2013 at multikulti, 18mm, Sigma SD14)

If you want to do a portrait of yourself you will want to use a tripod and timer for the shutter. Set at 10 seconds should give you enough time to get in position. Set the position like on a chair and have a friend or relative sit in a similar position as you and then zoom all the way into either their eye or just under their nose and set the focus on that surface and zoom out and frame for the eventual photo. This technique of focusing is also used in direct portraits.

Most cameras with timer will have a series of beeps every second and when the beeping speeds up that means you have 2-3 seconds left to be in your desired position. You can also set a burst mode of so many frames to get a series of photos and pick out the one you like the most.

Light, Photography Understanding and Practice by Jason S. Page

The End